Sonnets from a Floating Life

by

Don Moore, Jr.

"Sonnets from a Floating Life," by Don Moore Jr. ISBN 978-1-63868-044-4 (softcover); 978-1-63868-045-1 (hardcover); 978-1-63868-046-8 (eBook).

Library of Congress Number on file with publisher.

Published 2022 by Virtualbookworm.com Publishing Inc., P.O. Box 9949, College Station, TX 77845, US. ©2022 Don Moore Jr. All rights reserved. No part of this publication may be reproduced, stored in a retrieval system, or transmitted in any form or by any means, electronic, mechanical, recording or otherwise, without the prior written permission of Don Moore Jr.

CONTENTS

INVOCATION AT DAWN	9
INVOCATION BEFORE SLEEP	10
ROLLING	11
BLISS	12
WORMS	13
DISSOLUTION	14
THE PAVILION	15
DEVOTION	16
ANTS	17
SUBTLE TONE	18
THE SONNETEER	19
WORDS NO, PICTURES YES	20
SELECTING THE INK	21
SPIDERLINGS	22
PARAMECIUM PROGRESS	23
A DAY IN LATE SPRING	24
HYPERESTHESIA	25
RUNNING IT	26
A PICNIC	27
QUINTESSENTIAL MOOD	28
TRAGEDY	29
A MORNING DUTY	30
THE JUNGLE SONNET	31
POETICS	32
THE WHITE SONNET	33
ISOLATION BEAT	34
EVERY MINUTE	35
THIRTY DEGREES LATITUDE	36
THE LITTLE THINGS	37
GLIMPSES	38
THE AESTHETIC STYLE	39
THE PSYCHOLOGICAL STYLE	40
THE RELIGIOUS STYLE	41

THE CASUAL STYLE	42
THE SET-UP	43
NO GROUNDSWELL	44
THE HAUNTED PIRATE	45
WILD	46
PENTAMEROUS SEDULITY	47
FORTY SONNET MAN	48
THE LABORATORY	49
PATIENCE	50
SKYLINE	51
THE VAMPIRE	52
SUNK IN SPRING	53
DISORDER	54
A LADY'S VOICE	55
THE WOODS	56
IMMINENCE	57
WE'LL CALL ON POE	58
THE PLACE OF LEVERAGE	59
CATNIP	60
A NEW TACK	61
LABORIOUSNESS	62
T'AO CH'IEN GOES HOME	63
ENUMERATED RESOURCES	64
DEVINE DECADENCE	65
MEMORY BREAKER SONNET	66
TURN THE BLUE TO GOLD	67
DREAM SONNET	68
THE BOY	69
I ASK	70
PRAISE	71
THE GLADE	72
AFFIRMATION	73
AT HEIDELBERG	74
RIDING IN A CAR	75
MOOD MASTERY SONNET	76

MAGNET SONNET	77
MYSTERIOUS CALM	78
THE BLUES	79
SENSITIVE TO SOUND	80
A DOSE	81
BACKDOOR MAN	82
THE CHOICELESS BLUES	83
THE BACKLASH	84
BAD LUCK	85
DRIFT AND DREAM	86
THE U-TURN	87
MOMENTUM	88
KAMCHATKA	89
THE CUTTING EDGE	90
THE UNIVERSAL I	91
FLOW	92
A POEM ABOUT ENDYMION	93
TICK TOCK	94
POETIC TALENTS	95
THE MUSE	96
DEPTH AND DETAIL	97
TAKE IT AWAY	98
VALENTINES ON PARADE	99
THE FOURTH DIMENSION	100
POSSIBLE MONOMANIA	101
CHRISTMAS EVE	102
NEXUS	103
TO APHRODITE	104
TWO HERDS	105
ROLL THE JUGGERNAUT	106
BLOCKAGE	107
SARANAGATI	108
LADY LUCK	109
THE ANTI-SCHEDULE	110
THE DISPOSSESSED ARISTOCRAT	111

PSYCHIC ENERGY GENERATOR	112
DREAM TALK	113
AUTUMN EQUINOX 1980	114
FROM CITY OF NEW ORLEANS	115
TO THE SOUTH	116
MISSING YOU	117
HAPPY BIRTHDAY	118
EXPRESSION	119
OUR FIRESIDE	120
BEAUTY	121
THE LAST NOOK	122
FLOWER OFFERINGS	123
TO CATHY	124
TO CATHY	125
TO CATHY	126
TO CATHY	127
AN ANAGRAM TO CATHERINE	128

INTRODUCTION

Don Moore was a talented author and chose various formats in which to write. Having penned previous works of poetry, he contributed articles of humor and interest to Mensa newsletters: La Plume de NOM, a New Orleans group publication, and later to Lexicom of Bluegrass Mensa. He was comfortable in the world of words, producing lyrics, poems, sonnets, witticisms, and limericks.

A self-taught student of classic English and American literature, Don delved into the personalities and lifestyles of masters he chose as favorites: William Shakespeare, Robert Burns, and Edgar Allan Poe. Even though his style was a reflection of their prowess, his thoughts and writing took him beyond imitation to capture a mood, or explore a scene, or trace a context, or define a feeling that poetry engenders. His humor and intellect are hidden among lines that are sometimes ruled by hyperbaton and other figures of speech.

INVOCATION AT DAWN

If every dawn that lights the eastern world

Would torch a blaze of love within my heart;

If all the meteors this black night hurled

Against the airy walls of earth's rampart

Would coalesce their energies in me;

Or if this globe itself would now explode

And parcel this my frame unendingly

To thicken out the heavenly milky road;

Then might I know the sweetness of the one

Whose presence poets plead for in their rhymes,

Whose left eye is the moon, her right the sun,

Who sports with boundless spaces and with times

   And who, at start of one of our small days,

   Might grant: one solitary drop of grace.

INVOCATION BEFORE SLEEP

If little death must overtake me now
And Morpheus drop down his sable shroud,
Grant me a moment while I make a vow
To banish from my consciousness the crowd
Of "did once do, am doing, and will do,"
For I am done with do's, have paid my dues.
And Dawn, when come to paint the welkin blue,
Will find it so, if I have the power to choose!
Yes, sleep must take me to an argent sphere
Where honey-bliss is all I apprehend;
Then wakefulness must find me free from fear
And focused on my one fond hope: to spend
    Each moment of a stay in space and time
    In the loving arms of this goddess sublime.

ROLLING

Molasses movement, slow and sweet it goes,

A silver something sliding through a deep.

Smooth as a sphere, through unctuousness it flows,

Through regions borderless as dreamy sleep.

A moon-like mass, it moves but is not heard,

Silent along a cycle with no wake,

No turmoil and no calming down, no word—

Save the wild sound one of your names might make.

If there's a cry, it's Love, no thing is sought,

As on it rolls, a riding but no car,

No carrier, naught carried and – no thought.

This is the realm of a wandering bliss-star.

   "I think, therefore I am!" Descartes did cry.

   "I won't, therefore I ain't gonna," say I.

BLISS

Take the cursed thing and with it all of

What the world's common ones have said I'd miss.

Take each crass object and then gently shove

It where old Sol don't shine. Go for the bliss.

And when that other malady, that fit

Of clever full-of-thought paralysis,

That idle idea packaged up as wit,

Rears up its ugly head, go for the bliss.

So standing ever closer here upon

The edge of an unfathomable abyss,

Where startling is the glance – suddenly, gone,

Plunging into an ever-streaming bliss.

   Though the whole hideous world should shout of this

   And that and that and that, go for the bliss.

WORMS

When clouds of yellow-gray have emptied out

Their bladders on the sodden ground below,

And a few paltry dribbles from the spout

Are all that's left to join the earthward flow;

Worms, long and slender, worms invertebrate,

Those soft and slimy, slow and wriggling worms,

From grass to pavement start to congregate

Until with worms that oozing walkway squirms.

I step around. They should stay in the dirt,

Though in their squiggling antics laughs abound

And even when bike riders make them hurt,

And that's the way it is. I step around.

   People are worms, the way they writhe and wallow.

   To do the same, here's a sure method: follow.

DISSOLUTION

A China vase is lovely --- till it breaks.

A little flower smells delicate --- till crushed

By a load of horse shit which lies and bakes.

A bird's hidden note sounds cheerly --- till hushed

By a bullet. Cream in white and fluffy

Beaten waves taste sweet --- till turning rancid.

A soft soft kitten's touch is luxury ---

Till creeping wetness signals what he did.

Such facts and artifacts may bend and break,

Scatter, fracture, and wilt before a hiss,

But that base hammer-blow with power to make

Me lose my stream of bliss has been and is

   Like Death macabre, like Death in grinning dance:

   The <u>dissolution</u> of the mood Romance.

THE PAVILION

A bamboo bed lies underneath the trees

In this red-roofed "Pavilion of the Pines,"

And as the rains to a half drip decrease,

My sleepy self from Morpheus untwines.

Within the little stove the charcoal glows;

Within the kettle bubbles build their towers;

Within these old utensils something flows ---

But it's the tea, now, which yields its subtle powers.

The infusion. And like a violin

I tingle waiting to be played upon.

Alas, I see my Soma cup has been

Lost on the forest track, somewhere unknown.

    A search like this will never be a bother.

    To start, one place is as good as another.

DEVOTION

Day follows night and night the burning day:

They tumble on, leap-frogging one another.

The wheeling stars now hold a little sway

Until the sun their paling light will smother.

Day, night, morn, noon, dusk, eve, and midnight black

Go flitting past me in a dreamlike motion.

Hours, days, weeks, months, and years roll by and back,

And each should multiply my past devotion.

If I could find that continuity

Which drains each moment of its manna dew,

Turns time and space to points through which flow free

All traffics on the cosmic avenue –

    Then I myself a point, would feel devotion

    Pour ever through me like a rolling ocean.

ANTS

In the rain forest teems the army ant.

By that last word is understood the plural;

For even if he wishes to, he can't

Be independent: he is Nature's churl.

He crawls in mass across the jungle floor

Looking a writhing carpet on the move,

A hungry rug, a groveling insect corps

That in a seething ball at night is wove:

They're arm in arm et cetera in arm.

The elders lick the larvae 'cause they're juicy.

The males mate with the queen. The females swarm.

This is the bug who follows so obtusely

    Secretions of the crawler just ahead,

    If made to circle, he circles till he's dead.

SUBTLE TONE

I have been to the hills on rainy days

And sat inside a cave behind the showers,

When the far vistas disappear in haze,

And a rain-screen drops, and all the trees and flowers

Liquid, melt in a gray-green melody

Of sight-sound growing from the forest floor.

Tone. Tone. Tone. Do come drifting back to me,

Even me, your departed visitor.

What is the smell of raindrops in the breeze?

Those liquid lattices of molecules

Retain vibrations of the seven seas,

And could I touch the extract of those pools,

    Its Hebe then would fill my subtle cup.

    I rub my fingers and I hold them up.

THE SONNETEER

If I am aught, I am a sonneteer
Who in some poem's enchantment is confined,
And not a prisoner of a low career,
That darling of the baseborn groveling hind.
That cannot be the mojo of my mind.
I'm sure the green frog of a little lake
Must find the red dust of the road unkind,
Feeling his journey there a sad mistake
And longing for his lily pad again,
His deep pool with her quiet silver soul.
It's such a pool where I would dip my pen
And let it lead me to a mazy goal;
    I'd take my pad and print in runes upon it
    An evocation of a state: a sonnet.

WORDS NO, PICTURES YES

A deep well, splash, and something falling in it.

Look later crawling out a hybrid thing

Whose metamorphosis at every minute

Is madness – is a wonder – is a string

Of images, and with no cutting edge.

Fugacious thing that cannot stand and fight.

Mere nothing that can never hold a grudge.

Creative beast that is no parasite.

I somehow see a kite that's broken loose –

A lovely flower – a face comes melting through –

A lady softly moving like a muse

Through wheat fields in a dress that rustles too.

    The sky, the flower, that angel face, the moon:

    They dovetail this eternal afternoon.

SELECTING THE INK

"What color ink?" – A question for the willow

From the old poet, whom mid-morning finds

Awakened from the drowsy season's pillow –

To search like an addict for poetic lines.

Black ink for hist'ry, sordid bits of fluff –

Which float down ages growing up as weeds.

Red ink for love and death and ritual stuff –

It's a mad tryst with vague heroic deeds.

And blue, swimming in blue, that drips all over

And paints our portraits in philosophies.

Stop! Cleanse the wine glass. Let the heart recover

The ambling pace of spring bear through trees:

   Set out the green ink. Bid the flowers come.

   At that, the willow bows and the bees hum.

SPIDERLINGS

My thoughts should be like tiny spiderlings,

Who live on dew and wait atop their web

For the East Wind -- the gentle wind that sings –

To balloon them off into the world of Mab.

Now tumbling tumbling unpredictable.

The orb web's order, intricate with gyves –

Gone. Hideous schedules, repetition dull,

Discriminating culinary lives . . .

Of this they're free and all because they're young.

I would be young and I would live on dew

And be in states of which our bards have sung.

I'll put on emblems and perpend the new;

   Kill habit, reason, and the reasoning habit;

   Go to the woods and be a leaping rabbit.

PARAMECIUM PROGRESS

One thing happens to him and then another.

The hairy paramecium is here.

He's all nose. He's madcap. He's his own mother.

He makes an ocean in a glass of beer.

Ride on a bubble, seahorse of a realm.

Eight seconds in the saddle: rodeo!

The tumultuous trip won't overwhelm

A life at all times dipped in vertigo.

Depth perception redundant in the deep.

Play, Paramecium, and dizzy touch.

Yes, you, an ephemeron, will not keep.

Nose into – what? It doesn't matter much.

   Of the animals, none has ever meant less,

   But none has been so casually relentless.

A DAY IN LATE SPRING

I had been cooped up all day, when the storm
Rolled with its clouds and thunder overhead;
I felt the barometric plunge transform
The air, even while drowsed upon my bed.
The big drops ceased soon after they began.
Fragrance-enticed, I opened wide the door
And gasped, while my eyes, outside my head, ran
To dive where sparkles lit the leaves galore,
As new sun crisped the water-softened sights,
And phosphorescence mated with the sound
Of water draining, which always excites
A birdsong – and myself to roam around,
   For freshness had distilled the lingering time
   And dripped all over Nature's paradigm.

HYPERESTHESIA

I climbed a willow one deep afternoon –

The gentle willow with her gift of grace –

Waiting, then went up, to catch at the moon,

Only to fall pell-mell upon my face.

The willow made me want to taste the sky;

The willow made me want to see the wind;

The willow made me want to glorify

The oddities that rush upon the mind.

Hedonics. Two-edged sword that must be fed!

I am cut down and my face in the dirt.

(If dirt had feelings, it too would be red.)

And all that remains is a mass of hurt

   And that significant strange smell of art:

   A poem branding itself upon my heart.

RUNNING IT

A hang glider requires a takeoff run

To gain air speed, to place its ponderous

Bulk in cushioning air, and thereupon

To head toward new continents of cirrus,

To circle in a thermal up and up

And hobnob with an eagle soaring soaring,

Be in a Chinese scroll without a top,

An ink speck high above the mountains touring.

Run it on out? For this why wouldn't one?

Because of demons hindering every step.

It's said that "a cruel angel flogs the sun."

Brutalized by this backlash, I have wept

    Because distaste for all this toil and strife

    Leaves me: a Brittany snow scene of a life.

A PICNIC

Fresh parsley and the aromatic thyme,

(The viridescence in potato salad),

Say that the summer solstice is at prime

And take us on a picnic. In the ballad,

True Thomas had his shoes o' velvet green,

And I would wear such shoes: The violets

Are tender and a heavy footfall mean.

Surely we'll romp as in the old vignettes

Where sprites would sprite away in innocence.

Remembered fantasy is memory's best,

A distant daydream of the South of France.

I'll blaze a trail of neurons to that tryst;

    Brain cells of seven years ago are gone.

    Rosemary's for those times no longer known.

QUINTESSENTIAL MOOD

Picture a garden pathway. Picture not

Its end: It winds forever like a string,

A string of pearls a giantess forgot

In a corner of her boudoir lying.

In a banyan tree with a bright red fig,

A woolly wild macaque sits like an icon,

Considering a branch which appears too big:

It's a ten foot reticulated python.

Bring bring bring prey and predator together.

Cling cling cling, monkey, to your branch and shudder.

Wring wring wring, snake, the life breath from another.

Sing sing sing, trees, of nature's bread and butter.

   As the snake the monkey, the forest him

      Strolling. An old log rots in half light dim.

TRAGEDY

'Tis cruel to put more burden on another;

Fourteen and seven-tenths the burden here,

Weight of the world all happiness to smother.

Gaze at that hanging "star-crossed" atmosphere.

Another place could have a pair of lovers;

Another set of despots beat them down,

Raindrops in a huge somber sky which hovers

Above a flood plain where the sensitive drown!

A happy turning point? A hollow sound.

What turns is a huge malevolent mass!

A vital choice? On a merry-go-round?

The heart's constricted by those rings of brass.

   So take your poison, say your <u>au revoirs</u> ,

   And "shake the yoke of inauspicious stars."

A MORNING DUTY

It's I who has journeyed here. The trees stand,

And have stood, rooted in concentration

Upon unfathomable depths of aged land,

While leaves speak in wild improvisation

Of a journey into the blue distance.

I take an object from my saddlebag.

Weighty, it has the lustre which enchants

But more of that same specked metallic slag

Whose minerals feed the trees – and make them wise.

Deep among old brown leaves in mottled gloom

I sit riveted by those jewell'ed eyes

Which perhaps, in that subterranean tomb

   Whence came the idol, shed tears waiting for

   These intense rituals of its worshipper.

THE JUNGLE SONNET

The jungle python wraps itself around

His prey, constricting, smothering, swallowing whole.

Here is his masterful expression found.

But when tricks of his world subvert his role,

He's dumb: On defense he attempts to coil

And strike though lacking venom in his bite

And plays King Cobra with his clumsy toil

To persevere at folly out of spite.

Mellow my jungle or I am that snake.

Taints of the age attack on every hand.

And I am much too weary now to fake

Efficiencies I'm unfit to command.

    Once, at thought of a French poet, I cried,

    Because, in the face of all this, he tried.

POETICS

Gazing into silent distance, I dreamed

A comet at the solar system's gates

Was a tear welling up, and laughing it seemed,

And the idea of getting into states.

The coiled spring of energy in deep space

Catapulted a possibility

Into my telescopic lens to race

Through ether that is blood, is sea, toward me!

As a groggy sleeper gropes – after what?

A deed he vaguely knows but cannot do;

Thus I tried to stare at that nebulous spot,

Focusing as it swam into my view.

   I spoke a thousand tears. My destiny:

   Turn them to pearls. My worth: fidelity.

THE WHITE SONNET

White cranes wing their way through autumn heavens.

He of the canoe and wild rice now stops.

Clouds sit quietly: white lace heroines.

Jack Frost, due tomorrow, lurks and eavesdrops.

Soon snow squalls will build winter's Taj Mahal,

Resplendent cenotaph for a mind's gloaming.

Whence and whither comes that echoing call

Of a wild goose, stuck and bewildered, roaming?

The brilliant mirror of the Hunter's Moon

Doubles the daylight on the mountain side.

Rabbits frolic; perpetual afternoon;

Their fluffy cottontails won't let them hide.

    Goddess – bending down – heaven – gently kissed.

    Sinking sinking sinking into dawn's mist.

ISOLATION BEAT

What planet is this? Grape arbors abound
And through my trellis of sonnets the sights
Are so much less compelling than the sound –
The deep-diving pulse and beat which excites
As it pounds and dumfounds, finally drowns
Him who awaits a bizarre cryptogram,
Idiosyncrasy of these mad sounds,
And jeers an aside, "The public be damned."
In courtyards opening on the city's perils,
In antique rooms where carpets still are thick,
In mountain belvederes with stars as heralds,
In the moonbeam realms of the lunatic,
    That's where one hears the sweet musicians play
    Their song, "You've got to hide your love away."

EVERY MINUTE

Mind, every minute, look to concentrate

As will one day the marrow of the stars

Caught up in some grand gravitational fate

Relentlessly, profoundly – and it scares.

Blue green and gray, the earth spins and I see it,

Though I can never count its many storms.

Blue green and gray, the grass grows and I'll be it:

A mood's a mood and there are myriad forms.

The good words, words of love, drive out the bad.

O tune me up a notch, you troubadours.

I feel the tinglings, heart to toe to head;

They burst like unexpected metaphors.

    Ashamed of common thoughts, I'll rendezvous

    Where Love's own laureled shamans evoke you.

THIRTY DEGREES LATITUDE

Three hundred sixty temples in the hills.

White fluffy clouds in water floating free.

West Lake swallowed Taoist magic health pills

Making Hangchow an immortal city.

Westward, high inaccessible for most,

Old Lhasa sinks, yak butter in the sun,

Its rites of passage now almost as lost

As in El Giza's stone oblivion.

A flattened note comes drifting from an ocean

Of jazz and ragtime – and the blues too – pour

Through New Orleans, stuff for a sweet devotion

Hand-sculpted with <u>largesse,</u> <u>finesse,</u> <u>l'amour.</u>

   A poet, part Creole, could use a break.

   Kuan Yun Shih had six years at the West Lake.

THE LITTLE THINGS

It certainly is the little things that count.

What a valuable credendum, in truth!

Such heart warming trifles are paramount,

Like nail in tire, salt in soil, germ in tooth.

I saw an eagle with a vibrant wing

Nailed to a barn door. Absurd torture!

Impossible! But to that image cling:

An aching for complete divestiture,

A heavy weariness as drip by drip

There builds a huge stalagmite in my heart,

Disgust with mobs of everything that slip

From gross satiety to reeking fart,

    And that which will this whole sick list pre-empt:

    That most useful of emotions, contempt.

GLIMPSES

I sit up nights hoping, since dreams are poor.

A naked ankle glimpsed behind a door,

Its jade pendants tinkling across the floor,

And the embodied scent of 'evermore'.

What will become of this on down the line?

Where is Chateaubriand and where his sylph?

A sadness intervenes. No anodyne,

No intriguing footnote on the bookshelf

Of my mind undoes the dark limits Fate

Has set upon my palsied energies,

Upon my tethered vibratory rate,

Upon this land itself – and mysteries!

   Putting the gray sadness to use, I seem

   To be "lost in the cobwebs of a spring dream."

THE AESTHETIC STYLE

Upon the fringe of some Sargasso Sea

I saw unnumbered shellfish count themselves.

Crustaceans there were, crawling – stupidly.

So down I drifted as a diver delves

When coral reefs are megaliths of sleep.

Artists are known to wake up suddenly,

Attendant on that work which they hear weep,

As if Pygmalion's ivory girl could cry.

But would her tears come salty to my taste

Where consciousness has wet a kindred spirit,

I'd build a coral palace that would last,

And all the passing fishes would revere it,

    Wherein I'd set herself – Beauty, the Fay --

    Now smiling at the ocean's castaway!

THE PSYCHOLOGICAL STYLE

The row house window overlooks the street.

An old horse plods by, then a gray sedan.

Children play kickball on shady concrete

Till seeing the Italian ice cream man.

As evening closes in, my eyes close in

Upon the old gas lamp soon to be lit.

Its wrought iron post takes my attention then

To where I stare like someone in a fit.

Twilight – wandering outside – the iron post.

I play some kickball till we all adjourn.

Spumone – fruity, nutty –has engrossed

Me and I see it melt and perchance turn

    A reliquary for a profuse mood

    Into a four-dimensional hyper-cube!

THE RELIGIOUS STYLE

Sequestered in this symphony of stone,

Cathedral Notre Dame above the City,

Up the spiral tower, I hear gargoyles groan

And echo them with my own cries for pity –

A boon dear Lady! Through the air a sylph

Or in this torch's flame a salamander

Sent palpable to prove this hieroglyph

In stone to be a physic and a wonder

To the world: Send me an apparition!

I do believe I could play architect

And build an edifice from just one stone,

Were it the brick of gold which the elect

    Have made the mold for every contemplation, --

    While all their deeds shower down in dedication!

THE CASUAL STYLE

A monk has a hut near the tomb of Chu
In the Tang-tzu Valley of P'o-yai. Brooks
Gurgle right along, watering bamboo.
He gave up a while back and burnt his books
There is contentment in the simple way.
There is a peace where only Nature talks.
There is a clarity where mountains stay.
There is a sound as bamboo's hit by rocks.
This monk's old robes relax to fit his form.
If he goes for a walk it's always nice
Even when omenless clouds build a storm.
The wise old owl's hoot contains no advice.
   Sitting on the Dharma with a fat grin,
   Philosopher extraordinaire: Hsiang Yen!

THE SET-UP

Some years ago, before our instruments

Had ridden roughshod through the solar system,

Man fantasized a Venus which presents

Nooks: velvet and clover. And he missed them.

Now <u>Earth</u> sweats under noctilucent clouds

And CO_2 is belched into the air;

In quicksand with their baggage walk the crowds,

Desire upon desire turned to despair.

Where is the breadfruit? Where the happy lunch?

The dreamy helpers in the landscape garden?

Tell me a story, sudden like a hunch,

Of once upon a time and let a bard then

    Leap headlong through this set-up with a whoop,

    Fulfilling old desires in one fell swoop.

NO GROUNDSWELL

There may be groundswells somewhere out at sea,

But still – for every tide that comes, one goes.

I'll have to tap some other energy

In this my little boat that only rows.

Jeweled garden of a Persian miniature;

Illuminated French and Celtic books;

A Moorish arabesque upon a door

To history's head – with Easter Island looks.

Gimme some tone, some color line and shape,

A glint from off these icebergs floating south.

Whatever drifts by, suck on like a grape

And swirl its energy inside the mouth.

   An animalistic input with each breath

   I have, and finally – get this – my Death!

THE HAUNTED PIRATE

Sinking out of reach: ordinariness.

A haunted aspect charging day and night.

True Thomas tapped a fairy – a goddess.

On tenterhooks I'm waiting for my sight.

On tenterhooks a cloth and woven out

Of many different skeins of poetry

To dry and set, this knowledge that's about

A life as solid as gold filigree –

And equal rare and just as delicate.

Catch but a glimpse of that dim fleeting world

And careless desolation is your fate,

The Jolly Roger is your cloth unfurled.

    Roam for your power, roam the seven seas,

    And from everything take – mysteries.

WILD

I, the poet, sit here singing my songs,

My songs over and over, back and forth,

Like an excited caged beast who belongs

In the wild blackness of the Dipper's North.

I say that Poetry is a feeling

And I possess enough of lyric bent

To taste a bestial newness when I sing

And bury my nose in some fresh kill's scent.

Calm down, my poems. The wind is on the lake.

Await the twilight time of subtlety,

Depths of reflection that the moon will make,

When, fearless and relentless, we may be

   Into the wild inconceivable hurled,

   The airy Ovid of a spirit world.

PENTAMEROUS SEDULITY

Relax your hands completely; let them go.

Breathe rhythmically and match that natural sound

With mental Hong Sau played adagio

As when a little zephyr is unbound.

You have two separate eyes; now let them go

Till sight on sight with shadows do compound.

Let the ears listen to the tabby show

Which the world sends as undefined background.

This idleness is pink and mauve and true.

Faith is formless, unimplicated mellow.

But should you really crave a thing to do,

Sleep with a laurel branch under your pillow.

   I say in high style (Height is what I'm stalking):

   "Now you're onto something. Now you're (not) talking."

FORTY SONNET MAN

Look here: I am a forty sonnet man

And claim quietus of Significance.

'Man of the Forest' is Orangutan;

At fingers' ends his fruit and foliage dance.

Nature provides; if not, then 'fare thee well,'

For everybody does just what he can.

To work for something makes that something hell,

So I'll behave a forty sonnet man.

There is no need for duty: I'm at ease.

And entertainment is just simulacrum.

As for events: mere metamorphoses.

Anxiety: a dithered way to take them.

    Look here, I'm anxious about just one thing:

    Having enough contempt for such waffling.

THE LABORATORY

One night I crept into a laboratory.

I'd been invited but my friend was out.

I'd hopes of hearing some medieval story

Of the <u>Lapis</u>. Slowly, I walked about.

Three test tubes leaked their vapors to this cell:

Magenta leered from one, eager to splash;

And Black, viscous black, sat loath to gurgle;

The third, gray slime, seemed livid from the lash.

A flame, an orange flame, persistent flame

Was busy gently licking underneath

Until with fluids boiling over came

Contortions and the fire began to seethe

    With parti-colored jets, with sparks – a show

    Yes! But the consequences, who's to know?

PATIENCE

As when a boy, upon an afternoon,
Has made the wind a playmate for a day,
Both whistling up an independent tune,
And he would ride it as a stowaway,
And when his kite, the kind that's colorful,
Tail-waving storyteller in the sky,
Has dived nose first too close to that brown pull
Of a sycamore and is caught up high
Like an arm behind the head gone asleep,
And when the boy now tugging, using his
Strength, now toying, his wiles, to make it leap
Free, spends two hours twenty minutes; such is
   Patience, the most beautiful of the good
   Visitations – and the least understood.

SKYLINE

Artificial light shines on these buildings,

Brick edifices stolid and dreary

In a line. They seem dirty and used-up things.

Their windows, eyes in a skull, cannot see.

How long have they accumulated dust?

Permanently reaching for the sky they stand,

Thousand-year-old eggs with ash and lye crust

And also their foundations are on sand.

Suddenly a tremor (gargantuan!)

Runs through the earth and all these things collapse.

The land, now level to the horizon's span,

Reveals the lightning of far thunderclaps.

    Even the trummerfrauen of Berlin

    Could never pile up that rubble again.

THE VAMPIRE

That full moon burning in the headlong night –
As if some twinkling stars had been amassed
And fused to make one tyrannous naked light –
Can summon tides, tides of the mind, ones vast
Enough to fill an addict's restless veins
As all the while he curses what he craves.
The thing that drives him on: <u>it</u> never wanes.
Each trip in quest of blood the more enslaves.
Dawn arrives for this foul thing of the night
As when a thinker, puzzled by some query,
In an odd moment of distraction might
Forget his problem totally, nor dare he
   Wonder what it had been, lest it come back
   A Vampire screaming <u>Life</u> in dire attack.

SUNK IN SPRING

Mix Dew and Champagne in the Tulip time.

Roll out the carpet: Buttercups on green.

Soft are the animals, and sweet their mime.

Clouds can come and go, and never be seen.

It was here, then, in the flickering green shade,

In the oceanic shade of the tree,

Wherein the little darting sunbeams wade,

That, with a start, I spoke some poetry.

A bird is chirping on the hidden limb.

A breeze unbidden ruffles one loose feather.

Another bird picks up the tuneful hymn,

Far madrigal that links the trees together.

    They nod and sway in soft successive motion

    Like undivision of some sweet devotion.

DISORDER

As things spring up, they are just what they are,

And all arrangements play upon the surface.

And then cosmetics cover any scar,

And the poem forgotten for a prose preface.

I saw a squirrel go round and round a tree trunk

To scamper out on each limb and then back,

As if, quaffing sap, he wanted to be drunk,

Old Lord of the Wood – in this cul-de-sac.

You know, once from Virginia to Missouri

A squirrel could leap and never touch the ground.

Gone is that tangle wild where he could scurry,

Where the soughing wind – where a poem – would sound

    Like some tumultuous ballad of the border.

    There's something hideously wrong with <u>order</u>.

A LADY'S VOICE

As soft as feathers is the lady's voice,

And I can simply fall into that mood

Where latitudes and longitudes of joys

Impose a grid upon the world for good.

The sound, like water, rolling all around,

It doesn't matter where it's headed to,

For like that liquid it seems somehow bound

Toward an immensity, toward the deep blue.

She speaks, and melancholy rises up

Like undersides of leaves turned by the wind,

Like mixed emotions in a farewell cup

At some wild border, border of my mind.

    She lulls me and she lures me and she leads.

    I bid farewell to Ethics. He recedes.

THE WOODS

So very easy and so very hard.

Poised for something good, in the poet's wood:

It's the long floating walk of an old bard

Away from all the tyranny of should.

Yet all <u>my</u> journeys have been merely hops

Of some malignant dwarf from grove to grove

Across the sands of ennui – and of hopes;

The heat o' the sun, cold o' the moon, above.

Caught in the trammels of a thousand moods

Against a thousand trivialities,

What home have I in the deep shadowy woods

Where a sole strange bird calls from the high trees?

   Do I know Time? Impingement is his name.

   But I still hobble on, though surely lame.

IMMINENCE

Angel Falls Zambezi soaking wet

There's plenty water plenty water spray,

A superfluity like Time – and yet

I felt the wells go dry beside Pompeii.

Old burlap bag of junk nostalgic scenes

And heavy armor on the Roman way

Are baggage left behind by what it means

To feel the wells go dry beside Pompeii.

With hands behind my back I'm strolling blue

Remembering some foreign holiday,

Waiting – waiting to look toward something new

Now that the wells went dry around Pompeii.

    When? and upon what? may a walker stumble…

    While far away I hear Vesuvius rumble.

WE'LL CALL ON POE

We'll call on Poe as on a paraclete

With sounds and symbols of eternal time

And stroll the dreary hills in bittersweet

And yellowed hazes of an autumn clime.

Linger, bees, and we will linger with you

Over a flower of nutmeg faded brown,

Over some tiny intense rendezvous,

Over the quaint typography of a noun.

Your lines outre, where might they make us float to?

We unencumbered, we undoctrinaire,

When Hesperus outshines the sun, we quote you,

Where moss has left its softness in the air,

    Where emerald lakes are earthy eyes that see,

    When meteors fall – ever so silently.

THE PLACE OF LEVERAGE

Most surely, I have never been a sage
But some amalgam-drifter looking for
A place to stand, a place of leverage,
Who showed up nude to see the tidal bore.
I had no clothes, no time to put them on,
Only desire and never place to stand,
Only desire to wrest a goddess down
To some ellipsis in this nether land.
I've had a feel for power in all these tides –
Mare, orbis, aer, ignis – endorphin-borne;
But let me stand upon a rock besides,
A place of leverage whence I won't be torn
    Like a grunion, like a snail, like a toy.
    Ever so much I want to be your boy.

CATNIP

The sound of hot bugs droning in the trees

Is too too much to even listen to.

It'll drift on, wailing sad symphonies

For the droning many -- and beleaguered few.

A dish of butter on a day like this

Might melt -- and then again might not. If so,

I'd float a pungent herb, garlic ywis,

And that intensely green catnip I know,

Into my yellow momentary art,

A pigment for a dry and toasted crust.

Each bite would have its liquid counterpart:

Red, that Burgundy both harsh and robust,

   A moat around a palace of sensation

   Reverberating its own T'ang quotation.

A NEW TACK

There are a million sonnets to be written,
Ships with huge sails extended in the wind,
But rounding the Cape of Good Hope I'm bitten
By the tsetse fly of magic of the mind.
'An orchid blooms on the banks of Lethe…' –
How long, how often, pondered I the line,
Turning its fabric inside out to see
What threads of sound and image would combine,
Over and over, mural on my wall,
One only wall in a six-sided room
Which floats, if I smell anything at all,
In a sea of relativistic perfume!
    Fuse me a sound-bomb to go blasting through
    With the cry of the rose-breasted cockatoo.

LABORIOUSNESS

Heavy the load and heavier yet the forecast

Of a rock that must be pushed and rolled uphill –

Dragged, tugged, snail-like inch by inch – till death (or past,

For Sisyphus, poor wretch, is at it still).

With molten metal and bare hands produce

A fork to eat potatoes five feet down;

To quench your thirst, from boulders squeeze the juice;

Ragweed for clothes, for shelter holes, hands brown.

Again and again and again and again.

Day after day, wear hip boots, wade through mud.

Comb haystacks for a needle; find a pin.

Get a hand pump and circulate your blood.

    Label it ordinary, this estate,

    For the quotidian precludes the great.

T'AO CH'IEN GOES HOME

The years accumulate it: real ennui,

When bootless repetition gags and chokes –

Finally. Then the creature seeks the sea

Of spiritus fermenti, where he soaks!

The warm fluid bathes those hideous boils

Collected from afar, on pilgrimage

To the packed shrine of self-inflicted toils.

Now he's come home to his own acreage.

There is a feeling that is more than doubt,

A funny, fatal, irony of inaction,

For one who's felt the paltriness throughout

The known world. Vanished then is all attraction,

   Save when a strange atmosphere bathes his portals,

   And he longs to wander with the Immortals.

ENUMERATED RESOURCES

Behind a driftwood come a thousand waves,
Driving it high and dry upon the beach.
Up in the sky, the way a bird behaves,
A multitude of thermals are in reach.
Under the desert sand lie dormant seeds,
Which a coursing cloudburst livens as it passes.
A sticky-tongued numbat on termites feeds;
His well-aimed slurps at last his lunch amasses.
A quantum congregation in each case –
Like a solar wind come flooding from that star.
And back of me these sonnets force a pace
Would lead me where your blissful visions are,
   As I this many-sonnet-ladder mount.
   But, by Olympus, I would fain not count.

DEVINE DECADENCE

A castellated abbey on a lake –

Yes I have seen it in the light of day.

A castellated abbey in a lake –

I have peered down and seemed to drown where sway

Its turrets and their shadows fitfully.

And wafting from those depths in soft assent

Comes a presence, and it comes velvety

And leaves me so divinely decadent.

Split realms? Pots of gold at rainbows endings

Beyond horizons where the every meet!

Tangles of weeds and flowers in random blendings.

The sedge and sugar cane are passing sweet.

    I now cannot the one the less esteem:

    I view them both as if they were a dream.

MEMORY BREAKER SONNET

I drift, and with me drifts the time: the time

And all the tide of blood that ebbs away

From a heart that has been base – and been sublime!

I see pale mists upon a lake of gray

And clouds enveloping a mountain peak.

They roll and tumble toward me where I stand –

Or where I sink: My fading will is weak

And would know nothing but this wonderland.

Dream on, thou dreamer -- how the sweet dreams roll.

Unfixed, unsteady, vague, and swimming by.

Theirs is a tide of bliss beyond control,

Like purple clouds along the evening sky.

   Break! Break! Break every memory apart.

   Shatter them to pieces – or break my heart!

TURN THE BLUE TO GOLD

The color Gold and wrapped in licking fire,
And blazing as Apollo's last attire,
And after, writhing in my chamber's pyre,
A giant censer's arabesque empire –
Gold! Making of the sky a starry choir
Whose molten notes I hear and they inspire
Me in rapt meditations to mount higher
Higher – and I do. That hue is my desire!
And then – across the wall – a shadow too
Creeps – from out the tapestries – no clue
To why it grows and why it <u>will</u> pursue
Me and enfold me – and it <u>is</u> dark blue.
    And has come pelting down the years of old
        To leave me screaming "Turn the blue to gold!"

DREAM SONNET

There are liquids, rare oils and distillates,
Which, put in basins full of water, swirl;
And their intense commingling generates
Cascades of gold and lavender and pearl.
And just like this should swirl my dreams about me,
And soft as Night the spaces in between,
When to the astral lands I turn devoutly
And see -- what I <u>on</u> <u>earth</u> have never seen.
Fluttering, there are other worlds than this,
Strung out like beads of dew upon a lawn.
I'll make that pearly metamorphosis
Until those dewdrops in the sun are gone,
    If Night comes silver-shoed again this time,
    If Night comes answering my pleading rhyme.

THE BOY

Wasn't there once a story of a boy --

A boy, a legend, or was it a dream? --

Who, not content with any sort of toy

And feeling for such things but disesteem,

Wandered about with eyes cast on the ground

Through park and field, forever looking lost.

Espying him upon his dreary round,

A woman – was she such? – there did accost

The waif, inquiring sweetly what it was

He searched for through the fading afternoon

Among the browning stalks of brittle grass,

And heard his faltering reply, "The Moon."

    That small boy's restless hand in hers she took

    And pointing upward said, "There, boy, there! Look!"

I ASK

Ah, make this old dull fellow see again.

Uncurtain these sad eyes and let them rove

To meet with playful molecules and then

To frolic in their dance of light and love.

Sprinkle the fascination of the sky

(Whose rolling constellations never cease)

On these four dreary walls to fill my eye;

Put Pegasus upon the mantelpiece;

Set motion to this furniture, each thing

A "think" forever rising, sinking, surging,

Like chunks of matter hurdling on the wing

Through distant galaxies till mixing, merging

   In some finale of a rendezvous.

   I ask as much as I adore, I do.

PRAISE

When Monsieur, dapper with his boutonniere,

Smiles; when he clasps his own hands greeting you;

When he extols his art, an auctioneer

Of offerings staged to please the public view;

When he sweeps forward, on his lips the names

Of artists, works, of critics, what they think,

And with consensus multiplies his claims; --

Then know for sure: These galleries interlink

With darkened warehouse regions overfilled

With dusty canvasses all X'd and torn,

With statuary dead, mouths stuffed and stilled,

In a long lifeless row – forgot, forlorn.

   At such a thought my sonnets do grow lame:

   Dealers in praise will also deal in blame.

THE GLADE

The leaves had formed a fluctuating veil

Of light and shade and dancing greenery,

Dancing themselves, unstirred by any gale,

Beyond, beyond whose curtain I could see

Long dizzy arches of the flowering weed,

Of thickets bordering on endless paths

Searching out pools to wet the marshy reed

Or waterfalls where nymphs might take their baths.

And I was magnetized and pulled into

The wild adventures of the beckoning glade,

The deeper going then the deeper flew

The almost incense-riding serenade

    Of her who through the silver mists sang, "Bard,

    Focus your all on me and me regard."

AFFIRMATION

I see a mountain pierce a cloudy rack

Whose paleness mingles with twice whiter snows,

Mighty abode of the poetic act,

Where the immortals are, and where heroes

Must labor long with no substantial air,

Must grapple with foul brutish-headed guards,

Must guide their steps by intuition's stare

And mark their oneness with the gods and bards.

So I will live without an atom's air

And unperturbed make ugly monsters flee;

I'll sit with Sybil in her Delphic chair

And recollect my immortality.

   "That which I seek, I am!" How sweet a mood.

   Wait! It takes a goddess to make a god.

AT HEIDELBERG

Sunday, and the warm sun has claimed his day.

Yet mists afloat from night laze on the river

To mingle up the hill with the town's gray.

The Rhine flows by. It seems the antique giver

Of Heidelberg's rich hue-of-ages look.

And here I am – no, Morn has <u>found</u> me here:

Days past, the glare of memory forsook

The antechambers of the too severe

(And now tottering) castle of my mind.

Such light as I can see is: sun through mist.

Such stirring as is memory, the wind

Wafts my way, and one that <u>will</u> <u>not</u> <u>desist,</u>

   So deep it thrills, it throbs, in me its spells:

   The far melodious tolling of a bell.

RIDING IN A CAR

Mute is the brittle picture of a day,

A day I see outside this moving car.

The sky looks heat-hazed: it just seems that way,

Since the still autumn landscape stretches far

In tans and browns and golds. The window's closed,

And objects all sit ponderously along

The ribbon of the road, as if still dozed

From the low hum of some long-faded song.

This crazed inanimation rivets me,

Me, who rides not to, -- no more -- but away;

Who would renounce; who is a refugee;

Who has not one sole hope left in this day:

    Glued-up; poised; staring; now in tears -- for see.

    Agggh! A single leaf fall from an old tree.

MOOD MASTERY SONNET

I will be master of the several moods

That stalk the world as clouds the night sky ride,

Killing the storied stellar magnitudes,

Reviving one for every one that died.

Repentant tears of Cassiopeia

Drip on a passing cloudy handkerchief,

And I with her see her Andromeda

Chained to a rock in baleful disbelief,

There both of us float on the misty wave,

Whence soon we feel a presence hideous;

Draco the writhing dragon. None to save

This helpless maiden. Where is Perseus?

    Could there but be a celestial sword for me?

    I'd stab a serpent far across the sea.

MAGNET SONNET

Turn me to a magnet in the morning;

Absorb my senses as I do in sleep;

Make my straight spine into a polar thing

Around whose length electric currents sweep.

Vermilion – til I reel – bright red my blood;

Thus let it surfeit with such oxygen

As fans a fire of Hindu sandalwood

In the windswept Mountains Himalayan.

Raise all my energy from low to high

And rouse each nexus on the way withal,

For bursting from them like a butterfly,

Rich private worlds will make me Beauty's thrall,

   As if Horaijima, isle in the sea,

   Had again somehow surfaced magically.

MYSTERIOUS CALM

A dilatory summer darkness theme

Has laid its lassitude beside my table

And let me wander through the shadowy cream

Of the night's lacquered leaves and tender sable.

I entered something that was far away,

That etched the mirror set behind my eyes,

That will return again, a roundelay,

As Perseid meteors will in northeast skies.

I'd wear a myrtle chaplet in my hair

If I were predisposed to anything

Besides this longing sympathetic stare

Into the depths of what can only sing.

    Here will I stay, while still my heart doth beat,

    Eternally young, eternally sweet.

THE BLUES

A mastodon's ghost frozen in blue ice:

Such is my initiative. A boulder

Poised in mid air and sickening in size:

My destiny. Nothing good will occur.

A million Greyhound buses end to end

Won't reach a planet which is any good;

So I'll just trudge on foot around the bend,

Head cross country, and get lost in that wood.

O, dogged and driven, I'm dogged and driven.

The smoke from burning trash got in my eyes.

I feel so weak; I need adrenalin –

Which the night's evil readily supplies.

   It's said somewhere 'to run from pain <u>is</u> pain,'

   But these blues just keep falling down like rain.

SENSITIVE TO SOUND

The genius of a place is in its sound,

As subtle as the midnight pheromone

By which the lovely female moth is found,

As rhythmic as the blinking lantern shone

By Lady Firefly in her patterned dance.

Lead me. Lead me where that Love reigns supreme,

Sounds of the subtle rhythms and the trance.

In moonlight hear deep water bend the beam;

In sunlight hear the music of the motes.

Listen to exudations of the air,

To that something which through the tall pines floats.

If alchemy would let my atoms share

    A resonance when sounds begin to stir

    Of Love, then – But the big cats <u>never</u> purr.

A DOSE

Siderosis, from pumping too much iron,

(That repetition of banality),

Needs medicine, demands an anodyne,

A cure for superficiality.

So I've looked at books: Rumpite Libros.

Invoked the bards: They did the most they could.

In music, tea, and scenery a dose.

Wrought images that bold before me stood.

I'm ever left with two things, two quatrains,

And never see the sestet of my world.

Look rather in your eyes, hear plaintive strains

The blues haunting the air and sinking swirled

   Into a place where lights and shadows flit

     Unconsciously, where it's asked: What is it?

BACKDOOR MAN

Inside his house the average fellow lives.

He feels stupid. He comes out the front door.

He gets attached then to whatever gives

The promise: You will reign proprietor.

Things work! He feels <u>La</u> <u>Gloire</u> in all its rush!

He writes a book about positive thinking!

Things don't work. (Quite the opposite.) They crush

Him. Now it is with <u>Malice</u> that he's stinking.

Another breed of cat will stroll out back,

Will blithely stroll into a nothingness,

A nowhereness, a non-arousal, lack

Of all except a gliding – effortless –

   Until, turning his head, he sees all this,

   And, when the wind comes around, blows a kiss.

THE CHOICELESS BLUES

These blues seem to have just crept up on me.
They used no force – and not a bit will I.
I'll watch like watching whales swim in the sea,
Awareness which nobody can deny.
Man, social predator, an old hyena,
Grist for the mill, is only worth a laugh,
Or else in tears Hinnom become Gehenna,
And left untapped the profound mine itself.
Easy easy raindrop globe and goddess,
We're Piltdown slow inventing fire and bad.
O make a myth of what is just a mess
While Robert Johnson plays those blues so sad.
   I would do something, but when I begin,
   An incorporeal sadness hems me in.

THE BACKLASH

There is a deep sea diver who goes down,
A portion-rider on the reefs of life,
Not free, no, a hard hat thing, lead, who'd drown –
If I could reach his air hose with my knife.
This is the beast of fathoms – wavering graves –
Lover of murk and rattling through the mud –
Of algaed stones and tumbled architraves,
Peripheral fish and cold-congeal'ed blood –
A clutching creature with a mouldering skull,
Bringing up jetsam as a sick man barfs –
Phantasmagoric dredgings each and all
Into my boat – with nightmare-muffled laughs.
    Septic revulsion! This is what I've felt.
    Tempered Toledo steel hangs from my belt.

BAD LUCK

There are, and have been, creatures on this earth
Without the taste for tattoos or the pluck,
Who nonetheless see (ending their self-worth)
A brand upon their foreheads. This: <u>Bad</u> <u>Luck</u>.
The mirror broken and the stream undammed,
A raccoon sensitizes little paws.
Hooray for Evolution! Now renamed,
The creature mocks old predators because…
Sweeping out of some insufferable waste
A desert whirlwind finally drops its sand;
Figs even appear on bushes to taste;
Birds play music; and there arrives off hand
    A god whom no one can identify
    In shape of trees at dusk against the sky.

DRIFT AND DREAM

Do you know what it means to drift and dream

And grapple with nothing, nothing at all,

Like the buoyant ball afloat in the stream

Or the wind-borne leaf from the live oak tall?

An oyster has its shell: we have this planet,

Things six of one, half-dozen of the other.

Work surely will improve the realm – or can it?

There is an energy which asks…Why Bother?

Above the foam I see the cypresses,

The moon; feel in the river's undertow

An undertone; hear what the ebbtide says;

And with it to whatever ocean go.

    Embarked among the flora sublunary,

    I have one escutcheon: <u>Error Attentare</u>.

THE U-TURN

I ain't walkin' down this sad road no more,

Loaded, stirring up dust, about to choke.

There's no need to rehash that traveler's lore

About getting a black cat's bone for luck.

I'm doing a U-turn – and ambling back,

I hear the wide-eyed spaces in the trees,

And smells! Of these the landscape does not lack:

It's like a soft wind blowing through swiss cheese.

Impressions come from somewhere – they don't stick.

Who hoards the fragrance from a thousand miles?

Into a vacuum wonder rushes thick,

The integration of a thousand smiles.

   Noetic ruminations never keep well:

   'Twas rotten thinking about other people.

MOMENTUM

The usual sun rose, then went red giant,

Dense the cover, memorial of heat.

And I myself rocked back and forth, back and…

Forthwith I'm shaken from my petty seat.

Imagination metaphoric, ride!

Take one chord only from the classic lyre:

That unity of mood which takes the tide

In a catamaran pure and on fire.

I've seen the moon rise in the west because.

I've thrilled to the activity of stones.

Intuition has rubbed up against laws

Better left buried in haunted flute tones.

   The greatest weakness of the human mind:

   To stay within the confines of the known.

KAMCHATKA

There is an outpost somewhere far away,

Remote and frontier enclave of a fringe,

Kamchatka where a strange Romance holds sway:

It is from here I entered on this binge.

Voluntary or involuntary,

This being driven into a corner?

Where life has grown uncluttered as the sea,

Where one deep question only can recur.

The other poesies bloom and die away.

Sometimes a little Alpine Strawberry

Though, tastes delicately of yesterday,

Or <u>jamais vu</u> arrives for company

   While I wait on this barren ground unsewn.

   This is the last place before the unknown.

THE CUTTING EDGE

When all your dreams are pusillanimous
And all your ruminations niggardly,
When all your acts bespeak punctiliousness,
No longer in Kamchatka do you be.
Ugh. Mammal chased tail. Him got turned around.
Him upped and walked away from where he was.
It must have been the waiting on that ground,
That barren ground – and those motionless days.
Tears are crystal and the past is sundered.
Look at the Ceremony of the Tea.
For wherever wherever I've wandered
It's just that place itself calling to me.
   I dream a cutting edge, aciform, steel,
     Glistening – ready to sculpt, to reveal!

THE UNIVERSAL I

Open the sky and rain some planets down.
Throw Magellanic dust into my eyes.
Reap the wild stars that eons back were sown
To flower out some long lost paradise.
Explode what paltry cosmos in my head
Thrives on significances that are – less
Than one simple dream, or a bout in bed,
Mere light, or faint stirrings in the Loch Ness
Of my soul – if applicable. O there
Is something going on called operation,
And I would fain evolve (without a prayer)
Toward manifesting it, sans motivation,
    Till every utterance, each new quatrain,
    Bespeaks no circumscription of my brain.

FLOW

Take it all in, as easy as the Dawn

Glides miles and miles igniting drops of dew,

Or as the Dusk with no more than a yawn

Melts in a Shadow-pot the old to new.

The waterfalls of incandescent isles,

Where sunbeams ride the drops in golden glow,

Have no more pageants than with which beguiles

This little place right here my sense of flow.

Did I say sense? It is a multitude –

A bevy for a bevy. Take it in.

And all the rearrangements which are viewed

Come tumbling as creation genuine,

    Where there is nothing gained and nothing lost –

    Rimbaud turned a factory to a Mosque.

A POEM ABOUT ENDYMION

Once upon a time a mighty poet

(Plenary in potential, snuffed by Fate)

Upon the Latmos of his fancy met

That shepherd-prince who'd tumbled passionate

Into the Moon's long low and languorous beam;

Who thrice – in water, sky, and cave – had won

A tantalizing sip of his one dream

And craved the cup. Such was Endymion.

When merrily the poet interwove

His twice a thousand couplets, left alone

Eleven lines sighed <u>they</u> were not in love

And to the lyre gave plaint in bitter tone:

    If you that state of pure delight deny

    To us, watch out! We care not if we die.

TICK TOCK

Eighty-six thousand seconds in a day!
And each as like the other as the drops
Of rain that patter down upon the bay.
The water joining water never stops.
Now I could name these drops and call one Ralph
And give the little fellow aught to do,
Spurn many more, a few draw to myself
And make with comely ones a rendezvous.
And, let me see, if I could link some up,
Their force would fret a channel in the shore,
Making canals through its untidy slop.
Me! Alter the earth's crust! And furthermore…
   But my hot head the drops cool with a hiss,
   All made of the same stuff: essential bliss.

POETIC TALENTS

There is a myst'ry on the driven wind
Too subtly spoken for my callous ear,
When oaks nod and the wistful willows bend –
Even though I sit still and squirrels come near.
There is an arcane rite, I feel, here too
In the give and take of all their chattering,
Noise to an artful ear but talking true
To bards in flight upon an Orphean wing.
Eight million species and insentient powers!
Across the years I now should know them all:
The cryptic silence charactered in flowers
Or secrets blared out on the screech owl's call.
   Stupid to these, my hopeful mind descries
   A mystery that lies behind closed eyes.

THE MUSE

Lo, since the start of beginningless time,
From inner space three visions have combined,
Drifting and floating and swirling sublime
Round circumpolar regions of my mind.
A moon – I cannot say – that's risen gold
Or silver both, and bathed in red pearl too,
And on a salt sea shimmering manifold,
Cooling wild waters with the lunar hue.
And there, I sigh to say, a goddess is
With long hair gordianed up and beautiful,
Now bright, now dark, as moonbeams strike or miss
Her face and neckless made of human skulls.
   This thrills me so that I cannot but choose
   To kneel before the great Primordial Muse.

DEPTH AND DETAIL

At Sonnet One I commenced to study,

And at Eighty-nine I knew where to stand.

Negation, make me tolerant and free

To wield the cutting edge or wave my wand

In affirmation – worship – of that Beauty

Who whispers that she carries all the Cosmos.

At dawn or dusk I rise: hardly a duty.

Are there petals underfoot from Spring's lost rose?

What ritual was never done before?

You know, Elizabethans used to still

Such flowers to scent an ornate boudoir:

The smell is sensual, red, and volatile.

   As for me, to interweave this last line

    I'll float Sweet Woodruff in my breakfast wine.

TAKE IT AWAY

Sonnets, like Cognac from insipid wine
Double-distilled, come on and come again.
On board, the water at the Plimsoll Line,
Let's go down slow, us and our heroine.
To learn the Mississippi is a task:
In poetry, each has his private river.
A touch of grace has been the boon I ask
In mad infatuation for the giver.
The destination? Outside time and space,
Those ultimates of massive lock and dam.
I've pulled up at that river's Crescent place
Where in their trance the jazz musicians jam,
    Because I heard ol' Buddy Bolden say,
    "Funky-butt, Funky-butt, take it away."

VALENTINES ON PARADE

Once upon a time there was a good boy,

Like a good dog, whose friend was a nice kitty.

But up and down from East to Illinois,

Then South, they wandered – to the Crescent City.

They saw some maskers. It was Mardi Gras,

When Fancy fleshes out the poorest frame.

Freaks, fairies, clowns, and demi-gods they saw;

Fish, animals, and odds & ends they came.

Then at some aggregation magic hour

Unmasking put that motley krewe to rout.

The cat and dog, in deference to this power,

Also tried to unmask, but they found out:

    Theirs were no costumes; they could not depart.

    And the whole wide world beat like one big heart.

THE FOURTH DIMENSION

Columbus died; the world went back to flat.

And so it seems, a waxwork bad and bland,

Till something else, a depth, shines out of that,

When Leisure stretches out her soft right hand.

When Leisure stretches out across the days –

Like a languid cat upon a cozy rug

Whose fixed green eyes take from the wild fireplace

Immensities of some primordial drug.

There have been moments – but they weren't so styled,

For <u>Time</u> was not the fourth dimension there –

When stars dripped metal, or a flower smiled;

When turmoil and machines turned debonaire.

   Perhaps the mind, in any neighborhood,

     Can click into a matching region-mood.

POSSIBLE MONOMANIA

My brain, she's no longer a cauliflower.

She's a thin flat pancake devoid of taste,

Unagitated by the sweet and sour

So even condiments are just a waste –

And here is how the whole thing came about.

The Opus. I was trapped in a position

And wanted nothing more than to get out,

Until that thought only <u>without</u> <u>volition</u>

Had superseded every other thing:

A monomania in very deed!

And one, hammer and tongs, exhibiting

Such neural circuits of compulsive need

   As will allow another juggernaut

   To roll – when flower-bedecked that car is wrought.

CHRISTMAS EVE

The gray clouds mingle with the coming night
And chimney smoke turns wispy like the day.
Stray flurries gather round the one street light
Where people and their high-hat snowman play.
Inside, the fireplace beckons. The dry wood
Crackles and animates that red and green
Which long ago the Holly understood –
When the old horse with the yule log was seen.
Now up from the hot red mulled wine fumes rise,
And they are heady; while, beneath the tree,
The presents wait in colorful disguise,
Quite tipsy in their bright expectancy.
    Then, from a crystal object darts a glint:
    Two tiny skaters in an ornament.

NEXUS

Equality is not one of my wants:

Therefore I shall not study hoi polloi.

But calling forth a goddess _is_ – and haunts

My reveries and is my chief employ.

For sure she must dwell in some rarer plane

Where opalescent wavelengths pulse and shine;

And I believe the gateway's not the brain,

But in some nodal point along the spine.

So when I reach for something, I reach down –

An inquisition for an occult nexus –

Where curious feeds on the unknown

With all the energy and interest sex has,

    To seek this calcite shrine of superstition

    And give to pleasure different definition.

TO APHRODITE

O Aphrodite, I am ignorant

And crave instruction in the Art of Love.

An absolute immersion's what I want:

To slip beneath that famous Sea of Love.

So let the saline waters inundate

Those shells that lie in beauty on the beach,

And I with them. Once more they'll coruscate

When the ebb tide takes water out of reach.

I can't bend over to pick up these shells.

I hear the water and I watch it move.

I long for inundation by those swells

That ever animate the Sea of Love.

    O foam-born Aphrodite, make me true:

    To squander no emotion but on you.

TWO HERDS

I thank you Aphrodite for this love.

Your young bow boy had done a job on me.

And yet I fear that this great gift may prove

A fire of straw. The reason: energy

Lost lost in stupid unpoetic words.

I ask the boon of their destruction now.

And to this end I beg a pair of herds

Which my own labors never could endow.

I'll be the drover for these animals,

Then like Apollo trade them for a lyre.

I'll see the world as your Olympic halls,

Luxuriating in fulfilled desire.

   Here then is what is needed to appear:

   Fifty female pigs and fifty male deer.

ROLL THE JUGGERNAUT

Roll the Juggernaut for every treasure,

The copper coil that turns inside your head.

Roll the Juggernaut in every leisure

Moment. "Manifest me now," she said.

I start to ask the boon of luck and laughter,

Those antidotes to everlasting do,

And neatly armed, I hope to crank up after, --

As if <u>neatness</u> at a dump were apropos.

What a dump! So roll the Juggernaut;

On this one only thing be resolute.

The dynamo makes pictures passing thought.

Attract the Adya with an involute.

   There is a magic summons and it's this:

   Three strange objects appear from an abyss.

BLOCKAGE

O Aphrodite, I bring adoration

And really need to see you right away.

I do not like historic information

And much prefer a private holiday…

I thank you for that answer: I'm too tense,

And so I'm shut out from the subtle good,

Or should I say my brain's defective, since

Vaso-constriction starves my legs of blood.

You'd think that winter threatens frostbit feet

Or that I'm on a polar expedition,

The way I let a reflex obsolete

Commence this sanguinary inhibition.

   Eyes also suffer from this malady.

   If there came a vision, I couldn't see.

SARANAGATI

Saranagati. I can go this far:

Accept what's happened, tune in to what's next.

A further step: refusal to refer

To so-called facts externally annexed.

Saranagati. Now let's go down slow.

Opinions. They have all been set adrift.

Desires. They swing like signboards to and fro.

Their ultimate fulfillment is your gift.

But is the growing sense of relaxation

A cause or an effect upon this path?

I'm slowly coming to the realization:

Total relaxation is total faith.

    Look, now a goddess from the golden days

    Begins to metamorphose my gaze.

LADY LUCK

Who acts on my behalf? My principle.

What is this principle but Lady Luck?

To meet the Lady is quite possible

And by her beauty to be wonderstruck.

The cortex with her vision may be flooded

Or with opinion. Now what is your choice?

Opinion is a Nessus shirt that's blooded.

It kills your energies and hence your joys.

It clings as it caresses, but it kills.

Voluptuous desire is less a bind.

At least no web of vindication fills

What shortly may become The Empty Mind.

   And then your principle can rearrange

     This thing or that, or make in you a change.

THE ANTI-SCHEDULE

The prisoner clutched the rail, his knuckles white.

Some simple words he heard: "guilty" was one.

And then the sounds grew louder with his fright,

For the final sentencing had begun:

"To be hung by the neck until dead."

And he went wild and rushed outside and rent

The air with howls and in his anguish said,

"Get it over with!" His name was Moment.

Another place, another time, a lazy

Cloud drifted by. Reflected in a pond,

He soon got tangled in the blue-green maze of

Branches, and being not a little fond

   Of freedom, stared at the sky with regret

   And then just waited till the sun had set.

THE DISPOSSESSED ARISTOCRAT

To what should I liken thee, O my past?

To a totally eclipsed moon I liken thee.

For both I know are there, but overcast

By shadow, and their light is lost to me.

So wherefore am I here, this place, this time?

Sweet-singing Ovid, exiled from his home

To savage Tomis for a silly crime

At least could see the Moon, and she saw Rome.

A wistful longing steals into my heart,

Like autumn's breeze through the red apple tree,

For every promise ever made by art,

For the mad secret of my history,

    For one blown kiss reclaimed from paradise.

    Traumatic bafflement is in my eyes.

PSYCHIC ENERGY GENERATOR

I would not have ambition's images

To be the constellation 'round my head,

But send me things that I would never guess,

A hypnagogic potpourri instead.

A huge and heavy flywheel made of stone

Turns, and it builds up momentum, and it

Spins upon the right, and the copper one

The left side, and I watch them as I sit.

I pinch the copper stopped; the stone one whirls.

It generates this psychic potpourri,

Projects the jetsam of remoter worlds,

And the whole shebang is free and easy.

   Your nudity is openness askew.

   Open up and see what's coming to you.

DREAM TALK

The Himalayan Jay-Thrush, male and female,

A life-pair living love in their own way,

Compose duets among the trees to regale

And recognize each other through the day.

This is precisely what we two shall do,

An easy thing for those who talk with plants,

Though as of yet we have no mountain view

As have those feathered Creatures of Twin Chants.

Material that filters down in dreams

Or mantles through the natural world that's wild

Becomes the stuff that through our thinking streams

To recreate the Eden of a child

   Or that lost world of bunny rabbits – deep

   In the woods. Help me find it in our sleep.

AUTUMN EQUINOX 1980

Tired as a porcupine who presses down

The grass under a tree whose leaves are gone,

I welcome autumn in a mood of brown,

While birds fly off into oblivion.

As a youth, I went up to the capital

To serve the Emperor. Now I'm unfit

For poetry – except when the miracle

Of meeting you offers blessed respite.

You yourself are a blossom that once wilted.

The wrong soil can ruin a flower's growth.

But what remedy can be afforded

When a desert stretches before us both?

    Sleep may come, but only in nightmares dressed,

    Until rivers flow eternally west.

FROM CITY OF NEW ORLEANS

To dream with Cathy is a dream to me.

A kiss to "Love & Kisses" from my room.

These words must buck the mighty Mississippi,

Like Salmon who only need to come home.

Bayous and backwaters – I saw a fish

Standing up, crying, looking for his way,

And with a stare that might come from a dish –

Without you, I'm a stranger and a stray.

Oasis town! The levee made it that,

But I am sinking 'neath a cresting wave.

Your absence from me made the levee flat,

And so, until you come, I only have

    Japanese lantern days in quicksand ooze

    And nights that play the darkness like the blues.

TO THE SOUTH

The red rain falling will be – peach blossoms,
And not what Zion clouds precipitate.
Banished immortals' footprints, sage-poets' home,
Dreams of ghostly geniuses: all migrate
To the South – and such a toast will echo
Rippling through the champagne of the morning.
In blossom-showers the people happy grow
To birdlike in the after-rainbow sing.
So on my way I'll send back birds of passage:
They'll write you vernal letters in the sky.
And as you watch and read my constant message,
Just punctuate each couplet with a sigh
    That lovers ever have been separated,
    And that all things – even the winds – are fated.

MISSING YOU

How much I missed you no one would have guessed,

When next to me was just a window's sky.

I saw Arcturus rising in the East

And four stars called the lion leaping by.

Where is the kitty who will play with me,

As those four sparklers play with Jupiter?

By Jove, we do it much more cuddily,

And you're a kitten who knows how to purr.

We'll prowl by day and make our nest at night

When the moon turns our eyeballs into fire;

I'll lick your face, be careful not to bite,

Or let long whiskers be a painful briar, --

   And in a furry roly-poly tangle

   We'll recompose that sky which the stars spangle.

HAPPY BIRTHDAY

Wake up, it is your birthday, sweetest one!

A day between a double rendezvous.

For I have sought in sleep's oblivion

Those dreams wherein I go: crazy on you.

Meet me in the meadow in the morning

When galaxies of dewdrops wax and wane,

Where cuddly bunnies to the dawn's light bring

That love which makes one being out of twain.

Or meet me sitting on a golden throne

Clothed in a costume of diaphanous pink –

Or be the nymph upon my Helicon

So I eternally forget to think

    And on your birthday can such daydreams chance

    As steal from opiate Night her deepest trance.

EXPRESSION

Yes I speak English -- but that tongue is dull
Which moves not as a river to a fountain
To bubble over when my heart is full.
Not work nor help to scale Parnassus Mountain
Avails me now, for I would <u>float</u> up there,
A visionary lost balloon – insane –
Oblivious to all that is life here:
That "very simple unmysterious pain."
Then would we know states worthy of expression,
Torrential snow-melt gushing from our throats,
As the heart's fire unlocks our sweet suppression
And every poem would sound these constant notes:
    Love as we stop awhile, love as we rove,
    Wake up with love and go to sleep with love.

OUR FIRESIDE

A glowing fire as evening fades away –
Fades to a night of shadows deepening –
Shadows of shadows -- and the tall trees sway
Outside our hearth where the burning logs sing.
And deepens more the night, which has no end
As never ends our deep woods to the eye;
And the flickering embers ever lend
A strange abstraction and a memory –
Of nothing. Warmth has made an ambience
Entire itself in red and glowing gold,
Ecstatic mesmerizer of our sense
Of quiet coziness, of stories told
    Whispering, the wild wind, the stars above –
    And wonderful and all our own: our love!

BEAUTY

Beauty with you is most an astral thing:

The soft down-streaming of a cool moonbeam –

A dove light-hovering on a gentle wing –

Dawn, cushions, rosebuds, water, and a dream,

A dream I spoke about some time ago,

Recalling, looking at soft cambric clouds.

It is a place where our own movements blow

For breezes as we ride where all the crowds

Are green reeds in a hydrofoil so light

It barely brushes them. – But oh the color!

With daisies is the rolling hillside dight,

And never had I dream with their hues fuller.

   If both of us upon such Beauty draw,

   Our love can never be a fire of straw.

THE LAST NOOK

The stony surface of this mundane globe

Fluctuates, as a windowpane puts forth

A crystal fabrication and cold robe

When Boreas comes blowing from the North,

Then sees the sun flood it to nothingness

So that the effort may begin again.

And so, the two of us gild Nature's dress

And you a pretty floweret therein

And I a painted butterfly who would

Forever flit about his dainty dish.

That dress will fade and be discarded – should

It be – the earth turn back to stone – I wish:

    That there remain some nook of meads and lakes

    Where I may frolic with my Cathycakes.

FLOWER OFFERINGS

If all the birds that ever nested here,
High on our swaying silver maple bough,
Where winds a moment turn the green veneer
Of leaves to lightness and then back somehow –
If all these robins and their feathery kin
Would leave their worming to the fishermen,
Leave chicory seeds to blow off down the glen
And mites to hide themselves in bark nooks – then,
They'd notice in the nearby cottage there
A girl who is a goddess, spreading love
Around her, and the birds would fill the air
With happy songs and shower from above
    The myriad velvet petals of the rose
    Which, drifting soft, would at her feet repose.

TO CATHY

At budding time the oak puts out his leaves
And for these playthings squirrels adore the Spring;
Throughout the year another toy it gives
To the two-footed animals: a swing.
I seem to see it hanging in the haze
Of twilight, moving of its own accord,
As moves the wind of love down ancient days
Where fabled sweethearts whispered and adored –
In a soft grove – one soft as this I see.
A gorgeous girl now rides it, as this kiss
I throw rides on the ether floatingly.
Some operetta's dreamy stage it is
   And some ethereal beauty plays the part:
   That girl is Cathy and that swing's my heart.

TO CATHY

May every tree that sucks from mother earth

Her boons, her lifeblood, and her bension

Now shake unto the roots its barky girth

And cascade leaves from off its skeleton,

If such display might summon up for you

The nurture needed by a seedling life.

In rocks, bricks, chalk, parched earth with low gray view,

Grows nothing – and therein now wilts my wife

With min'rals may that soil grow manifold,

With copper reds and loams of chocolate,

An alchemist to turn the wheat to gold,

Where cattle in the springtime can graze fat,

    And where nearby we will make merry, we –

    Beneath a beauteous wish-fulfilling tree.

TO CATHY

If light could overwhelm me, I'd be down:
Your body glitters like ten million moons.
Or if tranquility admits of sound,
Your accents breathe a calm, like wind harp tunes.
Clad in lion skin, you roam the wood,
A favorite of the little creatures there,
Protectress of the weak, friend of the good:
The dainty flower, the tiny mouse, the hare.
At once as lustrous as the shimmering sea
And deep, deep quiet, all-encompassing,
You soothe. – I beg you, roam all over me:
Each cubic inch is my own offering;
    And so, of nights, beside your fragrant bed
    A boy kneels with a flower on his head.

TO CATHY

I witnessed once a chess game where the white

Had set his queen to regally command

With her pervasive eye from crown`ed height

The paths that wind across that chancy land.

Now his advance, to many a black pawn's sorrow,

Was as a romping boy's through meadows green,

Calling his dogs and running – till a horror

Spread wan across his face: He'd lost his queen.

Then he who'd checked was checked, was forced to send

Frail pieces out on desperate bishop's gambles

Or let a ravaged rock forestall the end.

I turned my head away, the board a shambles.

    It would be the same, Love, if I lost you,

    Who are my own heart's queen, fair kind and true.

AN ANAGRAM TO CATHERINE

O, I have been in love with twilight skies

When Venus, drop of molten gold, appears

To teach me of Romance's mysteries.

And I have waited as the bright moon clears

The east of day and those four winds that blow

Of every rustling duty and my mind

Of all but that one nightsong I must know

By now by heart, the goddess is so kind.

To face the brilliance of a mirror moon,

To be where all is one, where one is chief;

And when there stirs, besides the antique rune,

A wind, a leaf blows by – my life a leaf –

   And on that leaf an anagram so true

   Is writ: "O, I seek the real romance: you."